Anger Management for Women

How to Control Emotions and Let Go

By: Amelia Virtue

Publishers Notes

Disclaimer

This publication is intended to provide helpful and informative material. It is not intended to diagnose, treat, cure, or prevent any health problem or condition, nor is intended to replace the advice of a physician. No action should be taken solely on the contents of this book. Always consult your physician or qualified health-care professional on any matters regarding your health and before adopting any suggestions in this book or drawing inferences from it.

The author and publisher specifically disclaim all responsibility for any liability, loss or risk, personal or otherwise, which is incurred as a consequence, directly or indirectly, from the use or application of any contents of this book.

Any and all product names referenced within this book are the trademarks of their respective owners. None of these owners have sponsored, authorized, endorsed, or approved this book.

Always read all information provided by the manufacturers' product labels before using their products. The author and publisher are not responsible for claims made by manufacturers.

Paperback Edition

Manufactured in the United States of America

Amelia Virtue

DEDICATION

This book is dedicated to my mentor and best advisor ever Samantha. If it were not for here, my dreams of becoming a psychologist and getting one step closer to understanding the human condition might not have been realized.

TABLE OF CONTENTS

Publishers Notes 2

Dedication 3

Chapter 1- Anger Management- The Basics 5

Chapter 2- Anger- Causal Factors 8

Chapter 3- Anger Management Tips And Techniques 13

Chapter 4- Anger And Conflict In The Family 17

Chapter 5- Handling Anger In Children From An Early Age 19

Chapter 6- The Key To Anger Management 23

Chapter 7- Getting the Help You Need-Avenues 27

Chapter 8- Choosing The Right Anger Management Course 30

Chapter 9- Meditation 35

About The Author 40

Amelia Virtue

CHAPTER 1- ANGER MANAGEMENT- THE BASICS

Of all the emotions, anger is the one emotion that must be managed. Many a reputation and image have been ruined because of anger that was not managed properly. Anger has even broken up many families, relationships and even business partnerships. Anger Management is one of the hottest topics today. This is because more and more people are realizing that they need help with managing their anger. They want to acquire the skills and learn how to manage their anger. When you find yourself angry, you can try to change the mood with humour. For instance, if a conversation turns into an argument that makes you upset, make the effort to diffuse the situation using humour or wit.

Anger Management for Women

If you and your spouse often find yourselves becoming angry whenever you discuss something, learn to recognize when a discussion becomes an argument and then change the topic immediately. This can help you to control your anger or prevent your anger from taking over. If your child is being mischievous or unruly, leave the room for a moment and take a few minutes to calm yourself.

If your anger is triggered by your surroundings, change your environment. Go on a vacation or take off for a few hours for a change in scenery. If, for instance, traffic hazards make you angry every day, take the time to plan your route. Drive a different route.

If your child is showing signs of being unable to control his/her anger, help him/her change his/her mood. Look into what may be influencing your child's anger and the ways he/she is expressing his anger. Pay attention to what he/she is watching on TV or the Internet, what he is listening or reading in the papers and magazines. One of the best ways you can help your child control his/her anger is to lead by example. Show your child that you can control and manage your anger properly. If you are angry, tell your child you're angry and that you're going for a walk, for instance. This way, you are showing your child that there is another way he/she can manage his/her anger, and that he/she does not necessarily have to fight or express his/her anger in a destructive manner.

If you are the object of your child's anger, tread carefully. Tell your child that you're willing to listen to him/her but only if he/she is calm. This way, you are teaching your child to express his/her anger peacefully. If your child is angry, engage him/her in positive physical activities, play with him/her, draw pictures with him/her, listen to music together, etc. Teach your child to take deep breaths when they feel anger coming on or to count to 10 to calm him/herself down.

Anger Management Tips

In addition to the above Anger Management techniques and activities, there are some anger management tips that can help you during your time of crisis. Anger management worksheets can help you deal with your feelings in an organized, logical manner. While they differ in their approach and subject matter, the underlying theory behind them is the same. They can help you to recognize exactly how you feel and why. They can also reveal any negative tendencies you may have been using when encountering frustrating or threatening circumstances. Through careful self-analysis, they can help you to understand and prevent uncontrolled emotional outbursts. For many people, simply talking to someone about an infuriating situation is enough to calm them down. Anger is a complex emotion, and it may require trial and error until you find the technique that best suits your personality and circumstances.

In the next chapter, you will learn more about anger and the various factors that contribute to excessive anger.

CHAPTER 2- ANGER- CAUSAL FACTORS

There are many things that can cause a person to become angry. However, there are people whose anger tend to flare up rather easily for the most minute reasons. Some people get angry because other people disturb them in a way that is hurtful or painful to them. They tend to get angry if they feel that their dignity and status within the society are being threatened or may be spoiled. Discomfort can cause some people to become angry. There are those whose anger is triggered when they see any imperfections. People who have a tendency to give other persons unsolicited advice, often find themselves angry if their advice is ignored or not heeded.

Harsh words, insults and cursing can cause many people to become angry. This is particularly true if the harsh words or insults are aimed towards them. Think about a time when someone insulted you or called you names. How did you feel? You were most likely hurt, but you were also probably angry. After all, no one wants to be called names, be insulted or have his/her self-esteem trampled on.

Feelings of frustration can also cause anger. People get angry when they don't get what they want. In the same manner, people can get angry when they get something they don't want. It's the frustration of not getting what they desire that makes people get angry. There are people who experience extreme anger when they don't get something that they are desperate to have or own.

Situations and events can cause anger. For instance, small children playing noisily in the living room could make their tired mother angry when all she really wants is to relax for a few minutes and watch the news.

Anger can also be caused by psychological issues. People who are under a lot of pressure, are tense or lack a sense of humor tend to become angry frequently. If you feel like you cannot solve a problem, you are likely to become frustrated, which can lead to anger.

Even the rich people get angry when they lose. Losing some money may not put a large dent on their wealth, their anger is caused by the fact that they lost. People who are in pain, drunk, drugged or irritated can become angry. Many people also get angry when they are unable to communicate clearly.

There may be many things that can cause anger, but the two main causes are frustration and a feeling that other people do not respect you. Have you ever felt a little angry at another person because you didn't think or feel that he/she didn't care for you or respect you?

Whatever the cause of your anger, it is important that you learn to control and manage it because not doing so can affect your personal and work life.

Anger Is Based On An Inability To Resolve Conflicts

Anger towards others actually proves that a person cannot adequately communicate to resolve simple conflicts. Managing your emotional response is helped if you are able to resolve your conflicts amicably. Here are a few steps that help with conflict resolution.

Conflict resolution can be defined as eliminating or alleviating sources of conflict. It involves encompassing various conflict resolution styles that are intended to resolve conflicts by identifying the sources, and eliminating them. Conflict is known to have a detrimental effect on all individuals involved and thus such outcomes should be effectively resolved at the earliest stages before the conflict escalates and effects more than just the parties directly involved.

Avoidance

Much like the proverbial ostrich; burying one's head in the sand when there is conflict present isn't always the easiest option available. There are times when we feel obligated, particularly if it is a loved one involved in the conflict. However this approach can at times amplify a conflict and draw unwanted attention. This can then lead to issues such as embarrassment for the parties involved and often will hinder compromise. When there is a focus on a dispute it can be seen as weak to back down or compromise on an issue we feel strongly about. If you do feel it necessary to become involved in the conflict it is essential that you opt for a non-confrontational approach, regardless of your relationship with either party.

Problem Solving

While this may sound very simplistic, taking a simple approach to a dispute is often the wisest strategy. Rather than focusing on how the conflict is impacting you it is wise to focus on solving the problem at hand in a matter that works for all parties involved. When one of the parties involved in the conflict shows a willingness to work on the source of the problem itself, as opposed to just working for a better personal outcome you will find both parties become more responsive. Remember, only when both parties are open to solving the problem will you be able to start working on a solution. Often the initiator will be in a position of strength as they are able to shelve their own personal feelings to work on an outcome.

Amelia Virtue
Compromise

All conflicts will require some form of compromise if both sides are considered reasonable. In most cases, usually the end result is partial satisfaction for both sides, since both will choose to compromise and accept some middle ground. Compromise is essential for not only resolving the conflict as it happens, but is also essential if you are hoping to avoid the original dispute being an issue again in the future. Be aware that most reasonable person's intentions are stronger than their actual will and while both parties may agree to a compromise it must be sustainable for all concerned.

Accommodating The Requirements

Accommodating the other individuals' requirements is perhaps the most selfless of conflict resolution styles. Sadly while this will often be viewed favorably; it is rarely effective. One party should never take on all negative aspects of a dispute. This type of conflict resolution style will breed resentment over the longer term and will also set a precedent for future conflict. This is often the case when we witness bullying in younger people. When one side e.g. the victim of bullying (either physically or emotionally) is prepared to accept what is happening to him/her, it will set the wheels in motion to create a poor culture in either the workplace or social environment. Once this type of culture becomes established it is very difficult to change.

Separation

Sadly separation of both parties will at times be the only logical solution to conflict particularly when a conflict has the potential to escalate and impact others unfavorably. An example of this may be in the workplace where the needs of one may have an impact on many and an authority figure needs to take action to ensure a happy and productive work environment. This may also be the case when parents simply cannot sustain a happy environment for their children. While it is always the best course of action to exhaust all avenues of mediation, first there will come a time when the greater good needs to be considered.

Amelia Virtue

Chapter 3 - Anger Management Tips and Techniques

From mild annoyance, to full-blown bouts of rage, anger management techniques can help you understand and deal with this sometimes destructive emotion. Also known as "the silent killer", anger can devastate your body and immune system in addition to clouding your judgement. High blood pressure and high cholesterol, an increased risk of heart attack and frequent head and stomach aches are all symptoms of chronic anger. Learning to effectively deal with this emotion may actually save your life!

Anger Management for Women
<u>The Real Causes Of Anger</u>

You may think that the jerk who cut you off on the way to work was the cause of your road rage. Or perhaps it's the short-tempered spouse always blaming you for things which are beyond your control. The fact is that anger often stems from situations that cause frustration, disappointment, confusion and other negative emotions. It is a healthy emotion that helps us to avoid and respond to threatening or unhealthy situations. Controlling knee-jerk and confrontational responses to this otherwise healthy emotion, enables us to live a longer, less stressful life.

<u>Five Anger Management Techniques For The Home And Office</u>

Controlling a potentially explosive and destructive emotion requires identifying the root cause of the emotion and dealing with it in a non-confrontational, constructive manner. You can take control by following these five techniques:

- **Take a time out.** Knee-jerk responses are often the strongest and least helpful in dealing with the cause of your anger. Simply counting to ten or walking outside to get some fresh air can give you time to think about the situation.
- **Empathize.** Putting yourself in the other person's shoes can give you insight into his/her state of mind and allow you to take some responsibility for the situation.
- **Write it down.** Organizing your thoughts logically on a piece of paper allows you to vent some frustration safely and in a timely manner. You can let it all out without holding any punches.
- **Accept responsibility.** Admit that you had some small part to play in the situation that caused your anger. Did you communicate your feelings clearly and without hostility?

Taking responsibility for your feelings can be the first step in moving past feelings of frustration and helplessness.
- **Practice positive self-talk.** Did anything positive come out of this otherwise negative exchange? What are some of the positive ways you could deal with this situation in the future? Just saying these things out loud is sometimes enough to weaken any distressing feelings you may be experiencing.

Five Anger Management Activities

One of the worst ways of dealing with anger is to 'bottle it up'. This can be even more dangerous than emotional outbursts. In addition to identifying the cause of your fury or animosity, it's important to find a healthy way to express it. These physical activities can help you express your emotions and calm your body so you can think more clearly.

- **Breathe deeply.** Taking long, deep breaths helps to alleviate the panic that often comes with angry feelings.
- **Stretch.** Flexing your body increases blood flow and helps oxygen circulate through your body more quickly and easily.
- **Exercise.** Lifting weights, running or doing martial arts can divert your attention while still allowing a healthy release of pent-up emotional energy.
- **Do some housework.** Take out your fury on a dirty bathroom or kitchen.
- **Shout & scream.** If you have access to a private and somewhat noise-proof location, shout as loud as you can and scream at the top of your lungs.

Contrary to popular belief, it's not always best to engage in an aggressive activity to express your hostility. In certain individuals, these kinds of anger management activities can actually prolong and accentuate the negative feelings. Some studies have concluded that hitting a punching bag, ripping paper, or discharging a firearm may not be constructive methods of releasing anger for people with aggressive temperaments.

Chapter 4 - Anger And Conflict In The Family

While nearly everyone has experienced conflict in a work environment or socially, conflict in the family can be a different beast entirely. While it is true, familiarity can breed contempt, it can also allow relationships to slowly degrade over time with time being the actual catalyst. An example of this might be the parents of a teenager who feel they are losing touch with their child, when in reality the teenager may be losing touch with his/her sense of belonging as he/she attempts to establish his/her own identity, which can often be very different from that of the parent or role model. This might manifest itself as perceived laziness, to begin with and slowly evolve into something far more significant.

Identity is an important term in this context. As we mature we need to feel unique, and by very definition a family unit is a difficult environment for this to develop. Most of us do not appreciate change, as it makes us uncomfortable and in some cases powerless as we may feel we don't completely know a person as well as we may have previously thought.

Unresolved Conflict- Looking Beyond the Obvious

Often in a family environment there may be issues that are left only partially resolved and may arise often from a very small incident. This type of conflict can be the most difficult as you not only need to address the issue at hand but also understand the motivation behind a person's actions and how best to address them. It's only natural to avoid conflict but often avoiding the issue allows it to grow and gather momentum. It is impossible to suppress real feelings for very long and it is always better to get things out in the open before things get to a point of causing real damage to the family unit.

Role Models and Examples

Children will act out what they see, which is why a responsible role model is so important for the wellbeing of a child. However as parents with young children who may find themselves with far less time and significantly more financial strain this can often be the most difficult stage of life to remain composed and demonstrate effective conflict resolution. While this may sound simplistic, the solution is often to take a step back and take a more holistic approach. This takes discipline and an ability to understand the long term implications of one's actions.

Long Term Problems-Short Term Approaches

While this chapter only touches briefly on some of the causes of family conflict; as with any source of conflict there is always a common thread and that is the ability to not only see things from another person's perspective but also understand how it may impact upon them. This can be very difficult when it comes to families, especially parents who have raised their children with certain expectations.

The reality is a family will always have members in different stages of life. Experiencing different issues and having real empathy towards another can be difficult, difficult but certainly not impossible. Remember long term problems can be created with short term approaches to conflict. This is never more true than in a family. Now that we have discussed the family unit as a whole, the next chapter will discuss the ways in which anger in children may be dealt with.

Amelia Virtue

CHAPTER 5- HANDLING ANGER IN CHILDREN FROM AN EARLY AGE

Whether it's dealing with temper tantrums from a toddler or trying to calm down a raging adolescent, there are a number of widely-used methods of discipline that simply don't work. Over the past 40 years, several studies have shown with remarkable consistency, that anger management for children can rarely be accomplished with parental discipline alone. In fact, rewarding desirable behavior and punishing unwanted behavior are among the least effective ways to control anger in kids. In addition to your child's immediate environment, nutrition, exercise, sleep and leisure activities can all have a significant impact on his/her disposition and propensity to express anger in one way or another.

Anger Management for Women
<u>Dealing With Anger At A Young Age</u>

Kids spend the better part of their childhood learning about themselves and the expectations others have of them. Temper tantrums along with aggressive and violent behavior in children at a young age can lead to spousal abuse and an inability to express volatile emotions later in life. Before attempting to manage the behavioral expression of anger or hostility, we need to determine why a child is, in fact, angry. Misbehaviour can be a sign of other problems a child is dealing with.

For young children, inadequate nutrition can often be to blame for acting out and frequent mood swings. Too much sugar in the child's bloodstream can have dramatic effects on his/her emotional stability. In addition to hyperactivity and an inability to focus, too much sugar in your child's diet can also lead to crankiness and mood swings. For this reason, it's important to limit the amount of candy your child eats as well as ensuring that he/she follows a healthy diet.

Anger management for children also requires getting the right amount of rest. A sleep-deprived child is just as cranky as a sleep-deprived adult. Keep in mind that a child requires much more sleep than an adult, so he/she must be put to bed at a reasonable hour and given at least 10 hours of uninterrupted sleep a night. Just as sleep is required to charge their batteries, children also require frequent exercise in order to dissipate some of the energy built up during the day. Having your child go outside to play with friends not only serves to improve his/her sociability, but also allows him/her to expend energy in a healthy way which also reinforces healthy sleep patterns.

Watching too much television or playing video games, often can have a significant impact on the way children and young teens perceive the world and their place in it. Kids learn as much from fictional media, as they do from the real world. Prolonged exposure to violent images, profane music lyrics, and scenarios that promote or encourage negative behavior can certainly influence the way a child expresses his/her aggression. Restricting exposure to these types of stimuli and monitoring them yourself whenever possible will allow you to identify any possible negative influences they may be having. Spending time with a child engaging in coloring, painting or other artistic activities can allow them to express their emotions in a calm and productive manner.

ADHD & ODD

If, after monitoring his diet, exercise and sleep patterns, your child is still acting defiantly, with no indication of the source of his hostility, there may a deeper behavioral condition. Children with Attention Deficit Hyperactive Disorder (ADHD) can often be quite sensitive and have difficulty moderating their emotions. The extra energy in their systems can sometimes burst out in explosive fits of rage or aggression. Medication for ADHD can help control these symptoms, but it can also bring about strong mood swings when first starting or ceasing to take the medication.

Many children with ADHD also suffer from Oppositional Defiant Disorder (ODD). This is a pattern of disobedient, defiant and sometimes hostile behavior toward adults and other people which goes well beyond what is considered normal behavior. Children living with this disorder often argue with those in a position of authority, defy rules, annoy/bother others and act spitefully and rudely. While it is normal for children to display some of these traits occasionally, the child must continually display several of these types of behaviors in addition to meeting other criteria in order to be clinically diagnosed as ODD.

Anger Management for Women
<u>*Anger Management For Teens*</u>

A recent study by the US Department of Education found that during the school year of 1999 to 2000, 5.5% of school teachers were violently attacked by students and 10% of all elementary school kids who were expelled from school, were expelled because they brought a firearm to school. Adolescents are particularly at risk of developing anger control problems. Feelings of helplessness, isolation, and frustration combined with easy access to firearms and personal information have led to unimaginably cruel methods of bullying and torture perpetrated by students on one another. Anger management for teens is particularly important since the inability to control impulses, resolve conflicts and evaluate consequences can have disastrous repercussions. For adolescents, the right approach to anger management often doesn't involve disciplinary actions or lectures on appropriate behavior. Instead, demonstrating empathy for your child's current circumstances and discussing solutions in a forthcoming manner can go a long way in opening up a dialogue based on trust and mutual respect.

Anger management for children goes far beyond simple methods of punishment or discipline. Identifying the true causes of tantrums and aggressive or confrontational behavior often requires first eliminating physiological factors known to cause mood swings and anger in children and teens. There are excellent books and video courses for anger therapy, developed by noted professionals that can guide you towards insight and solutions to your particular situation. And while there are numerous qualified therapists and courses that cater specifically to anger management for children, any lasting changes to behavior rely on you, the parent, to see your child through these increasingly turbulent times.

Chapter 6- The Key To Anger Management

De-stress

Stress is a response to our life-time experiences. Demands made upon us often result in symptoms such as tightened muscles, pain, headaches, rise in blood pressure, release of hormones, and shallow breathing. Stress is not a physical substance we can place into a bucket, and is often created by our own thoughts and perceptions of life.

Disease is a result of stress and built-up emotions created by trauma or life choices. Stress is stored or remembered by our bodies in cellular memory. We each have the ability to change those old stresses from past events, if we choose to do so through non-invasive stress release and life-style changes.

Learn how to relax as a non-invasive choice to relieve daily mundane stress. Learn how to remain calm and peaceful during stressful situations. Re-educate cellular memory and muscles to reduce stress of past traumas or memories. Get to the root of the problem, instead of continually covering up the messages our body and emotions are providing us through symptoms of stress or pain. Change live-style habits and limiting beliefs to better care for yourself.

Stress can be physical, emotional, or chemical. The stressor can be real or perceived. Whatever the stress, it stimulates the body's natural "fight or flight" mechanisms.

Examples could be:

- Sore Muscles from physical exertion - work, exercise, gardening, etc.
- The long commute to work, travel, sitting or standing all day, poor posture.
- The stress of a job can be both physical & emotional - deadlines & quotas to meet, long hours, demanding boss, lazy support staff, late deliveries, complaining customers, etc.
- Relationships - They are difficult! Whether it is the kids or a spouse, co-workers or neighbors; relationships at times can take us to the breaking point.
- Chemical or environmental stressors come in many shapes sizes and forms, but the end result is always the same; they cause some level of harm to us.

These types of stressors can be, and often are, self-induced. These are usually habits that are completely modifiable such as; smoking, over-eating, drinking in excess, and the use of drugs. All of these stressors if left untreated for long enough will bring about a state of dis-ease. But what can a person do about relieving the stress in his/her life?

The Relaxation Response

The answer is simple. We can't all quit our jobs, leave our relationships, and move to the country. What needs to be done is to incorporate a simple stress reduction program into our lives.

History has shown the use and benefits, of many stress relieving techniques. These could be anything from meditation to massage, yoga to tai chi, body wraps to facials, exercise to nutritional supplements. Today, these treatments can be known as Spa Therapies. The point is that they all stimulate the body's natural "Relaxation Response". This reverses the harmful effects of stress.

Amelia Virtue

It has been proven scientifically, that a person who uses. Life is made to be enjoyed.

Here are a few massages that you can do to relax:

<u>Swedish Massage</u>

Feel the stress melt away with this relaxing massage. Long smooth gliding strokes soothe and pamper your body. The Swedish Massage also helps to improve circulation and enhance skin tone. Pampering yourself should be a normal part of your day. We all want the joy of living, but sometimes find it hard to make time to treat ourselves right. It's time to Spa!

<u>Deep Muscle Therapy</u>

This type of massage is ideal for chronic muscle tension. With slow intense strokes, and deep finger pressure, your massage therapist can relax muscle fibers and ease restricted movement.

Regular exercise is an important part of good-health, but sometimes too much of a good thing can hurt. With Deep Muscle Therapy, a specialized form of massage therapy, you can assist the body to recover from exercise induced soreness. Deep Muscle Therapy will help work out build-ups of lactic acid (a by-product of exercise). It will also stimulate fresh, oxygen rich, blood to enter the muscle tissues. This reduces recovery time and promotes healing. Exercise needs recovery time too

<u>Hot Stone Massage</u>

Enjoy a sense of total release as a specially trained therapist use warm, smooth Basalt stones to relax every muscle in your body. Described as being like having a massage in a whirlpool bath, this spa treatment is the utmost in luxury. The warmth of the heated stones helps increase circulation to the muscles and, brings fresh oxygen to the tissues. The density of the stone adds the perfect pressure to help release toxins stored in the muscles. The overall feeling of the massage is absolute bliss.

Chapter 7 - Getting the Help You Need - Avenues

Dealing with anger can be a full-time job for some of us. Whether it stems from frustration at work or the daily annoyances of family life; learning to deal with and prevent emotional outbursts can have a significant impact on your work and family life. Online anger management can give you the professional guidance, proven techniques and reliable support you need to effectively control your emotions.

Traditional Therapy Sessions

Face-to-face counseling from a qualified therapist has several benefits compared to other approaches. Your needs can be addressed immediately and your progress can be monitored carefully. Sessions are usually confidential so privacy and anonymity are assured. You can adjust the number and length of therapy sessions to fit your busy schedule and you can choose the therapist you feel most comfortable with. The biggest disadvantage with traditional anger management therapy is the cost. The bill for weekly sessions can quickly add up. If your therapist happens to live far from where you work or where you live, you may be stuck with a commute through rush hour traffic. These disadvantages have paved the way for a less traditional method of therapy.

Anger Management Courses

Online anger management is a growing field that teaches students how to resolve conflict productively, identify negative patterns of behavior, to release anger in a non-threatening manner. An experienced therapist can guide you through the course work at your own pace. You can join a class and participate in chat rooms and discussion boards led by a facilitator. If you would like more privacy and anonymity, you can also choose more focused one-on-one classes with a qualified therapist. There are also a number of reputable online anger management course providers that can provide proof of enrollment certificates and certificates of completion to satisfy any court-ordered or human resource ordered anger management.

DIY Anger Management

If you prefer a more flexible, economical solution for dealing with anger, there are also different approaches for guided self-study. For those with mild anger issues seeking to improve control of this sometimes destructive emotion, there are dozens of excellent books written by behavioral experts specializing in anger management. If you are prone to frequent bouts of rage directed at family members, coworkers, and friends, a more thorough self-study anger management course with ebooks, DVDs, emotion journals and other constructive work sheets may be appropriate.

Amelia Virtue
The Efficacy of Online Anger Management Solutions

As with most things in life, you get out what you put in. This is especially true when it comes to self-improvement. Anger can be an all-consuming, debilitating emotion pervading almost every aspect of your personal life. Not only is it fierce and unyielding, it is also complex and requires frequent introspection and analysis. Seeking to understand and control your anger in a practical way requires dedication and patience. Whether you enroll in an online anger management course or attempt a self-study method to control your emotions, the magnitude of improvement will primarily depend on the amount of time and effort you put in yourself. Of course it is important to choose materials and study methods written by credible experts that are appropriate to your particular situation.

CHAPTER 8- CHOOSING THE RIGHT ANGER MANAGEMENT COURSE

If you've never had a counseling session or attended a self-help workshop, you probably don't know what to expect from anger management courses. They can be attended in person at continuing education institutions and counseling clinics. Or they can be taken online in much the same way that you would complete an online university course.

These courses typically follow an established syllabus and work to accomplish several goals developed by the facilitator and/or the educational institution. In the past, there were simply blanket anger management courses that taught general strategies for dealing with anger. The increasing demand for specialized courses has given way to a surprising diversity of course offerings to fit your particular needs.

Court-Ordered Anger Management Therapy

If you have been ordered by the court to enroll in anger management therapy, you need to find a course that will be acceptable to satisfy the requirements of that order. You can do a search for courses being held in your area that will satisfy the specific requirements and the time deadline. Quite a few online anger management programs are also accepted by the courts in each state. However, before you pay for the course, it's a good idea to discuss it with your attorney who can give you a better indication of whether or not it will be acceptable.

The growing popularity and quality of online anger management courses allows you to satisfy a court order without having to arrange childcare, commute and rearrange your schedule in order to attend face-to-face sessions. In fact, many of the better online courses provide a personalized letter of completion and an affidavit form (signed in front of a notary) to verify you are really taking the course. The courses also have compulsory attendance and may require students to keep a journal, meet privately with the course facilitator and complete numerous assignments and questionnaires.

Anger Management Therapy For The Workplace

A happy, relaxed employee is a productive employee. Workers suffering from depression, financial troubles, parenting issues or general stress disorders can benefit from anger management courses offered face-to-face or online. As an employer, you can offer your employees access to phone and Skype counseling so they can receive the help they need from the privacy of their homes. If there are anger management facilitators available for on-site counseling, you can also arrange therapy sessions that fit the schedule of your employees.

Anger Management Programs For Health Care Professionals

Health care professionals operate in an especially stressful environment that demands positivity and friendliness from its personnel at all times. The demands placed on physicians in particular, can be extreme and unyielding. A growing number of anger management courses are being offered to prevent accidents, decrease employee turnover and instances of unprofessional conduct by health care personnel. These specialized workshops are available at selected locations across the country and can often be completed within a few days.

Couples Counseling

Anger Management for Women

Couples counseling may be court-ordered in cases of spousal abuse. However, it can also be quite beneficial for couples experiencing conflict due to difficulties communicating, frequent disputes arising from intimacy issues and arguments over work/financial concerns. These courses teach techniques for de-escalating arguments and preventing explosive outbursts. They also teach participants how to identify emotional triggers and turn the energy of rage into sexual passion. The emphasis is on building intimacy and improving healthy communication between partners.

Anger Management Programs For Adolescents

Depending on where you live, there may be workshops/clinics offering anger management therapy for teens and children. Children are living in ever more stressful times and often feel neglected and misunderstood. Acting out in anger may be a symptom of something entirely unrelated. An experienced facilitator/therapist can help your child increase his self-control, learn relaxation techniques and learn how to identify the underlying source of his feelings of frustration and rage.

Hallmarks Of A Good Course

There are plenty of good (and bad) anger management courses on- and offline. Choosing between them can be difficult if you don't know what to look for. The course you enroll in should be flexible enough to meet your time, financial and geographic limitations. Check the credibility of the institution and the course facilitator. There are numerous certifications recognized by the National Anger Management Association (NAMA) as well as degrees/diplomas in the areas of mental health, psychology, family therapy, domestic counseling, and various educational fields. Ask about the syllabus, course materials and methods of contact (face-to-face, chat, phone, email). A cheap course doesn't necessarily signify an inferior one, but inquire about class size and whether or not there are any extra costs.

Get Into An Anger Management Class Today

The most important thing an anger management class can do for you is to teach you how to control angry reactions in the heat of the moment. An angry reaction in the wrong situation can lead to damage being caused to property or to violent incidents which can result in permanent injury or criminal record. Controlling anger in the immediate situation is possible using techniques which will become more natural as they are practiced; such as counting up to ten and then back down again, or using phrases such as "these feelings will pass" or "these feelings are passing through me and are being released". Once a habit of using this type of technique is formed, and it becomes a conditioned response, dealing with anger will be so much easier.

Avoiding people and situations which stimulate anger is one obvious way of lessening the chances of a violent reaction, and this is obviously something you need to strive towards doing. Although it will not cure the underlying cause of the problem, it will give you breathing space in which to work out an effective and coherent plan, and it will also give your nervous system a chance to calm down and recover. This is not always possible, for example, in a situation where neighbors are causing difficulties, but it should happen wherever it is possible.

When you attend anger management classes, you will be able to practice using techniques which calm the body and emotions in simulated but realistic conditions. This means that the responses which you learn are far more likely to become ingrained into your habitual behavior patterns and become part of your response pattern. As well as using breathing techniques and phrases which can program the mind, you can also use yoga positions and soft music to bring calmer feelings. Portable audio systems allow music to be accessed in situations outside of the home.

Much of what is taught at an anger management class is aimed at helping you deal with this type of short term situation, but there will also be advice given on how to find a more lasting solution to the problem. Obviously, a large part of this will be making lifestyle changes to make you a generally more happy and balanced person. A great sense of freedom can be gained from finishing situations which have not worked out for you or from getting away from bad people. Cutting excessive alcohol consumption out of your life or even avoiding food with excessive stimulants can also help to create different behavior patterns over time.

The people running your anger management classes may also be able to put you in touch with professionals who can help you to deal with any long term underlying condition which is causing the feelings of anger. Often, there is nothing in the immediate situation which justifies the reactions that occur; they are stimulated by events of the past which need to be accessed under therapy conditions. A course of counseling can help to identify what it is in the past which is causing these difficulties, and hypnotherapy can certainly help to relieve it. Ask for referrals at your anger management classes.

Chapter 9- Meditation

No one meditates with the mind, but through the body. One comment I hear quite often is "with no meditation, I cannot focus my mind enough." In meditation, we are not "in the mind": we are focused on our bodies. The first part of meditation techniques for beginners is always an exercise in "making contact" with the body. It is an essential element of any meditation or relaxation.

Calming The Mind

The only way to calm the mind is simply stop using it. When you direct your attention to your body, your focus directs to a place that is not your mind, and that brings, naturally, a state of peace and relaxation. It is not theory, it is a practice proven time and time again when we do meditation in our meditation techniques for beginners center. You are not your mind.

We are so accustomed to using the mind constantly and compulsively, that we forget that the mind is simply a part of us and not who we are. The mind is a wonderful tool but it is just that, a tool. Ideally, when they need to, then turn it off.

When you do a meditation, you focus your consciousness (who you are) to a "mindless space" which many call your "Inner Self" – the person you really are. Eastern cultures are well aware of that state and what that space is, but we in the West have lost touch with that "Inner Self" that represents our true essence.

Why Turn Off The Mind?

When we fail to turn off the mind, the problems begin. Why? The reason is simple. The main function of the mind in our daily life is to solve problems. It's a matter of logic that if you are using your mind constantly, you need a constant problem to solve!

The result is what we know so well. We spent the day "going around and around" with things; analyzing situations, thinking and compulsive repetitive thoughts, focusing our consciousness on problems that need to be resolved. The "tricks" we use to calm the mind.

Meditation Techniques For Beginners

In our modern society we have created a series of "tricks" to calm the mind momentarily. We use them specifically to create distractions and shut out that constant "mental noise." One is the television. In the U.S. many call "gum for the brain." We all know that kind of "dumbing down" feeling after a while watching TV, especially if you choose a program that requires no intellectual or analytical effort (most). Another is alcohol and narcotics. Toxic substances inhibit the operation of the brain and, therefore, the mind. During the time that you are under the influence of alcohol or drugs, you get a "calm mind" simply because its organ, the brain, gets shut out.

There are also physical stimuli, mainly food and sex, sports, etc. These pastimes move away our focus from the mind to the body during the short time we are doing them. And at last, are the situations that trigger emotions in us. They are very effective ways to "stop thinking for a while." Watching a football game, for example. Meditation by Rennett Stowe under CC-SA Playing cards with friends. Driving at speed on dangerous roads, sport risk and, interestingly, consumerism ("I feel bad, and I buy something to feel better").

Of these methods, some are beneficial, others are simply pleasant and some are harmful to varying degrees of variation. But with all, the problem is that we use these "tricks" for a purpose beyond its purpose, for pleasure, fitness etc. We use them to do something we cannot do without them. Turn off your mind.

The Result Of These "Tricks To Turn The Mind"

- Instead of eating something good for the mere pleasure of eating, you do it to distract you from your problems. The more problems you have, the more you eat, leading to obesity.
- Instead of enjoying sex for the pleasure of the act, or as a way of showing love to your partner, it becomes a compulsive act of evasion.
- You spend all your income on consumer products to keep your mind distracted for the duration of the act of consumption.

The solutions provided by the meditation and relaxation

- When you meditate, you get distract or calm the mind.
- You get to focus your attention to a place within you that is not constantly analyzing, criticizing, etc.
- With practice, you get into a meditative state in seconds. When that happens, meditation becomes a powerful tool in your day to day life. You feel bad, and in a few moments, turn off the mind; you focus on your "Inner Self" and in comes peace.

Does this sound utopian? It is not. It is something that thousands of people get every day around the world and often we practice in our center.

What Happens In A Guided Meditation Tour

First, sitting in a circle with dim lights and soothing music, you are moments "by focusing". John Curtin's voice tells you all the time what you should do, where to focus your attention, and the steps to do so.

Next, we conduct a physical relaxation exercise. We focus on our body through breathing. Feeling your breath is a tremendously effective way to relax and calm down. You learn to breathe in a relaxed and deep way, inducing a deep state of physical relaxation.

Having achieved this state, guided meditation begins. During meditation, John Curtin guides you in a visualization process taking the form of a "virtual tour". Each display is different and usually has a specific purpose, depending on the "issue to be addressed" in meditation.

People who have some practical use these views to get in touch with your "Inner Self" and draw conclusions and specific messages on the subject to be treated. Others simply use the sound of the

Amelia Virtue
words to "distract the mind", thus gaining a deeper state of relaxation.

ABOUT THE AUTHOR

It was Amelia Virtues goal to study psychology at some point in her life and when she was offered the opportunity to do some research on anger management in women she could not pass up that opportunity. She was dedicated to the study and was able to learn a lot about how anger affects women and the methods that could be used to diffuse that anger.

Amelia was encouraged to write a book using all the research that she had compiled and that she did. It took a bit of time but, in the long run, it was one of the best decisions that she had ever made.

www.ingramcontent.com/pod-product-compliance
Ingram Content Group UK Ltd.
Pitfield, Milton Keynes, MK11 3LW, UK
UKHW022218230426
12048UKWH00016BA/915